Presidential Elections

Sherry Howard, M.Ed.

Reader Consultants

Brian Allman, M.A.
Classroom Teacher, West Virginia

Cheryl Norman Lane, M.A.Ed.
Classroom Teacher, California

iCivics Consultants

Emma Humphries, Ph.D.
Chief Education Officer

Taylor Davis, M.T.
Director of Curriculum and Content

Natacha Scott, MAT
Director of Educator Engagement

Fiction Author: Dona Herweck Rice

Publishing Credits

Rachelle Cracchiolo, M.S.Ed., *Publisher*
Emily R. Smith, M.A.Ed., *VP of Content Development*
Véronique Bos, *Creative Director*
Dona Herweck Rice, *Senior Content Manager*
Dani Neiley, *Associate Editor*
Fabiola Sepulveda, *Series Designer*
Lucy Zhang, *Illustrator, pages 6–9*

Image Credits: p4 U.S. National Archives; p5 U.S. National Archives; p10 top Shutterstock/Joseph Sohm; p10 bottom Getty Images/Rick Friedman; p11 top Shutterstock/Matt Smith; p11 bottom Library of Congress [LC-USZC4-1329]; p12 Getty Images/Luke Frazza; p13 Alamy/The Photo Works; p14 Alamy/Reuters; p15 top Newscom/UPPA/Photoshot; p15 bottom Getty Images/Kean Collection; p16 Shutterstock/Rob Crandall; p17 Shutterstock/Joseph Sohm; p18 top Shutterstock/Joseph Sohm; p18 bottom Shutterstock/Michaela Warthen; p19 Shutterstock/EchoVisuals; p21 Shutterstock/mikeledray; p21 bottom Shutterstock/Jillian Cain Photography; p22 Alamy/Jennifer Mack; p23 Alamy/Bob Daemmrich; pp26–27 Getty Images/Bettmann; p28 Library of Congress [LC-USZ62-13035]; p29 Alamy/Shaun Jones; all other images from iStock and/or Shutterstock

Library of Congress Cataloging-in-Publication Data

Names: Howard, Sherry, author. | iCivics (Organization)
Title: Presidential elections / Sherry Howard.
Description: Huntington Beach, CA : Teacher Created Materials, 2022. | "iCivics"--Cover. | Audience: Grades 4-6 | Summary: "Every four years, the United States elects a president. The country has gone through this process every four years since it officially became the United States. Learn about the people's right to elect leadership for their country and understand the role the people play in their democracy"-- Provided by publisher.
Identifiers: LCCN 2021054711 (print) | LCCN 2021054712 (ebook) | ISBN 9781087607160 (paperback) | ISBN 9781087630564 (ebook)
Subjects: LCSH: Presidents--United States--Election--Juvenile literature.
Classification: LCC JK528 .H68 2022 (print) | LCC JK528 (ebook) | DDC 324.973--dc23/eng/20211203
LC record available at https://lccn.loc.gov/2021054711
LC ebook record available at https://lccn.loc.gov/2021054712

TCM | Teacher Created Materials

5482 Argosy Avenue
Huntington Beach, CA 92649
www.tcmpub.com

ISBN 978-1-0876-0716-0

Table of Contents

Every Four Years

Every four years in the United States, a presidential **candidate** wins an election. This person becomes president of the United States! Sometimes, this is a new president. Other times, it is a current president who has been elected for a second **term**. After each election, the president takes an oath. The president swears to preserve, protect, and defend the United States Constitution.

A president's **inauguration** is a big deal. It follows years of hard work. The long campaign is over! Many voters celebrate the victory. Others may feel sad that their candidate did not win. In Washington, DC, many events are held to honor the new leader.

Ronald Reagan, the 40th president, is sworn in for his second term.

Barack Obama, the 44th president, is sworn in for his second term.

During the campaign, the candidates present their **platforms**. Voters study the platforms. They choose the candidate they think will govern best. Voters expect their candidate to keep the promises they make.

Once a president is sworn in, it's their job to work with other government leaders. It is also their job to represent the people. The president works for all Americans, whether or not they voted for that person.

Jump into Fiction

In This Thing Together

Kevin and Jay were best buds from the time Kevin held his new baby brother Jay in his arms. Kevin looked Jay in his tiny, button-nosed, and pucker-lipped face and said, "You and me, dude. We're in this thing together, all right?" And that was it. Best buds forever.

Even with ten years between them, they were always together. They wrestled and rode bikes. They had pillow fights through the house. They played catch and kicked goals, and Kevin was the one who taught Jay to jump the curb on his skateboard. "You and me, dude," Jay repeated. And Kevin gave Jay a fist bump and wrestled him to the floor.

Best buds for sure.

Of course, the older they got, the harder it became to do *everything* together. Jay could visit Kevin's college, but he couldn't go to classes with him. When Kevin and his friend Gina went to the movies, they didn't really want Jay around. And then, there was this voting thing. When Kevin turned 18 last summer, he registered to vote. But Jay was too young and not allowed to vote. Now, it was an election year. Kevin would get to vote, but not Jay.

Totally not fair, Jay thought.

"What's got you bugged, bud?" Kevin asked his sour-faced little brother.

"How come you get to vote and I don't?" Jay whined—just a little.

"Well, it's an age thing, bud. Only adults can vote. At least right now." Then, a light bulb went off for Kevin, and he knew exactly what to do. He grabbed Jay in a fake headlock and said, "Come on, bud. Let's figure this thing out."

Kevin opened his laptop and went to each candidate's web page. "Let's start here, bro. We'll learn all about the candidates. I'll cast the vote, but you and I can learn and decide together. How does that sound?"

"Cool!" replied Jay, tackling Kevin in a bear hug.

Over the next weeks, Kevin and Jay did everything they could to learn about the candidates. They read the newspaper and listened to debates, interviews, and news reports. Kevin taught Jay how to find reliable sources online, in print, and on TV. They talked about what they heard and saw. They listened to adults they trusted for their ideas, too. And then, they made a decision.

On the first Tuesday in November, the two went to the polls, and Kevin cast their vote. Jay couldn't wait to see who won!

Back to Nonfiction

Assessing Candidates

Politicians promise changes they will make after they win. It is up to voters to assess those promises. Are the promises what the voter wants? Are they within the power of the president? The president has limited power. This is because the president shares power with Congress and the Supreme Court.

So, how can a person find out what promises a candidate is making? Candidates run on platforms. Platforms, or plans for change, are public. They are posted online, mentioned in speeches, and talked about a lot.

Presidential candidates Hillary Clinton (above) and Mitt Romney (below) lead rallies.

PRESIDENTIAL DEBATE
TOPIC: THE SUPREME COURT
9:10 PM ET
CNN FIRST PRESIDENTIAL DEBATE
#Debates2020

People may also get to see candidates speak live in rallies around the country. They can watch candidates debate one another on television, too. People can learn a lot about candidates by their words and actions. They can also look back at what the candidates have done in the past.

Platforms and Mottos

William McKinley became president in 1897. A motto can be a short description for a candidate's platform. McKinley's motto was "Prosperity at home, prestige abroad."

Background Checks

When a company hires a new employee, they may do a **background check**. The media often provides such checks on each candidate. They tell the people all about each candidate's history. This will include details about their personal and public lives. There is very little information kept from the public. Candidates often share the details of their lives very openly.

If a candidate has a history in politics, people can check their record of votes as well. Voting records can give a good idea as to where candidates stand on issues. Voters can see clearly if the candidate's votes are similar to how they would vote. This may be a good way to judge if the candidate is the right one for them.

Presidential candidate Al Gore answers questions from reporters.

It is possible that some things a candidate says may not be truthful. Candidates may make a mistake when they speak. They might stretch the truth to appeal to voters. It is up to voters to make careful checks to see what's true. Checks can also help voters learn more about the candidates. Knowing about the candidates goes a long way in deciding how to vote. The more information the voter has, the better. Reliable news sources can help with these checks.

Fast and Easy

It is easier today than ever before to fact-check. People can use reliable sources online and in print. This is very different from the early days of the United States, when news was limited and traveled slowly.

Firefox   File   Edit   View   History   Bookmarks   Tools   Window   Help

https://www.factcheck.org/search/

FACTCHECK.ORG *A Project of The Annenberg Public Policy Center*

HOME   ARTICLES ▾   ASK A QUESTION ▾   DONATE   ARCHIVES ▾   ABOUT US ▾   SEARCH   MORE ▾

Search

is congress exempt from student loans?

Sort by: Relevance ▾

Student Loans - FactCheck.org
ss-not-exempt-from-student-loans/

s of **Congress**, their staffers and their family members do not have to pay back their
gressional employees are eligible to have up to $60,000 of **student loans** repaid after
al workers. But that's not the case for ...

Read the
View t

Donat

Think and Talk

What value can fact-checking sources have for people?

13

The Great Debate

People can learn about candidates in their public debates as well. Candidates can debate any time. But televised debates are big scheduled events. There are two types of debates. The first is within one political party. Those candidates want to get their party's nomination. The second is after each party has chosen a candidate. Those candidates debate one another in the months leading up to the election.

These debates are not required by law. But they are expected. Voters like to see the candidates compare ideas. They also like to see how candidates behave in a debate. The candidates might agree on some basic guidelines before debating. Some debates are calm and others are not. Some candidates speak well on camera. Some people do not do as well when put on the spot.

Elizabeth Warren (left), Joe Biden (center), and Bernie Sanders (right) debate in hopes of becoming their party's candidate.

presidential candidates John F. Kennedy (left) and Richard Nixon (right) in the first televised debate

The first televised debate featuring presidential candidates was in 1960. Seventy million people watched. Richard Nixon debated John F. Kennedy. Kennedy was known for his good looks and charm. Nixon looked uncomfortable on television. Nixon lost the election by a narrow margin. **Polls** revealed that the debate **influenced** voters.

Early Debates

Abraham Lincoln and Stephen Douglas debated seven times. They were fighting for a seat in the Senate. These debates are famous to this day. They helped launch the type of debating that is still done.

Voting Laws and Processes

Once people decide who to vote for, they are ready to cast their votes. Who is eligible to vote for president can vary state by state. How people vote also may vary. Even though the president holds office for the whole United States, states still have a say in how the vote happens. States may have different ideas about the best processes.

Voters check in at their voting location.

Voting Age

At one time, only people 21 and over could vote. That changed when the 26th Amendment became law in 1971. A big reason for the change was the draft into the U.S. armed services during the Vietnam War. Eighteen-year-olds could be drafted. People thought they should be able to vote as well.

Who Can Vote

There are two main factors when it comes to voting in a presidential election. First, a person must be a citizen of the United States. There is no way for a person who is not a citizen to vote. People who are not citizens can voice their opinions. They can go to rallies. They can support candidates. But they cannot vote.

Second, a person must be 18 years old or older to vote. When citizens turn 18, they can vote in the next presidential election. Most states require voters to **register** before the election. In some states, people who are younger than 18 but will be 18 by Election Day can register early. Information about how to register is easy to find online. In fact, many states allow new voters to register online. But these rules vary by state.

Voters wait for their turn and then vote independently.

Registering to vote today is much easier than it used to be. But it is not always easy for all people. Some voters have a challenge getting to the registration office when they cannot register online. Some have a challenge with online registration, too. Other voters cannot read very well. Today, people can get help if they struggle with any of these things. Citizens who speak a home language other than English can get help if they need it. Federal law requires that states offer them help. Ballots and directions are available in many languages.

Voters can register to vote in many ways, including at temporary stations such as this one.

Casting a Vote

If they meet the requirements, a person can vote on or before election day, depending on where they live. They may vote in person, and in some places, they may vote by mail. Some people may vote online, but that is very limited.

The most common way of voting is by casting a ballot at a **polling** place. Registered voters are assigned a polling place. During voting hours on election day, they go to that place and check in. They may be given a ballot and go into a private voting booth. They might fill in their ballot by hand, or they might use a computer or a machine to help. The way the ballot is completed depends on the state. Once they complete their ballot, they turn it in for counting. It might be deposited in a sealed ballot box or perhaps scanned in a machine. It will then be counted with millions of other votes.

sample ballot for president and more

Rules at the Polls

Each state has its own set of rules at polling places. In many states, people at or near the polls cannot wear shirts or buttons with political messages. In some states, people cannot loiter, or hang out, in the area after voting. In many states, people cannot campaign at or near the polling place. And in some states, they cannot ask voters how they voted.

Voting by mail is also an option in many places. Some people vote by absentee ballot. They request a ballot ahead of time because they know they cannot be at their polling place on election day. They might be out of the country or be kept from the polls for another reason. They receive their ballot in the mail and return it by mail as well.

Many states have also turned to a mailing system for all people. It is called universal vote by mail. Every registered voter in those states may receive their ballot by mail and mail it in before election day. Or they might deliver it to a polling place on election day. During the worldwide pandemic that kept many people home for the 2020 election, many voters opted to vote by mail.

U.S. citizens living in other countries usually vote by mail. This helps many military families vote.

Voting by mail has become more and more possible and popular around the country.

What the People Want

A strong majority of voters state that they prefer a vote-by-mail option. They like its ease and convenience of not waiting in line to vote.

Popular Vote or Electoral College?

People registered. They voted. The votes were counted. Simple enough, right? Not when electing the president.

The nation's Founders argued about how the vote should go. The Electoral College is based on their arguments. Many people at the time thought that Congress should select the president. After all, members of Congress were elected by the people to represent them. Other people thought that the people themselves should elect the president through their votes. They settled on a unique process to decide.

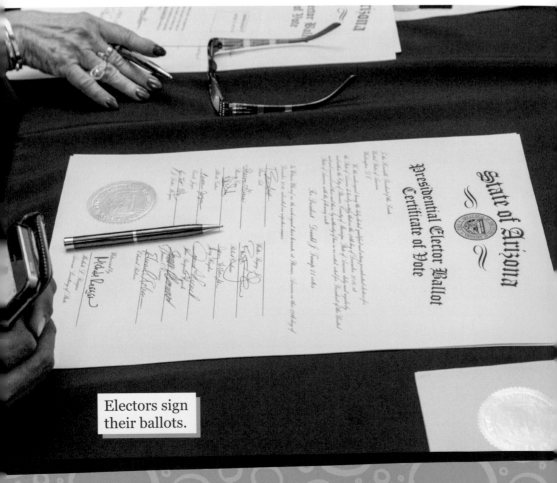

Electors sign their ballots.

The Winning Idea

The Electoral College was the compromise that won out, but it was not the only idea proposed at the time. Other ideas included election by Congress, election by state governors, election by state legislatures, and direct election by the people.

The popular vote is a count of each vote. One person equals one vote. The Electoral College is a process, not a place. Within the process, there are official electors. The number of electors in every state equal its members in Congress. The electors in most states are meant to vote with the majority of voters in that state. In some states, the electors are divided by percentages of votes. Either way, it is really these electors who cast the votes for president. The electors meet and vote in December after the November public election. Congress counts their votes in January, the same month the new president begins office.

An elector posts her ballot.

The Right to Vote

Keeping elections open and fair is a topic of concern for many people. Every election, there are people who voice concerns about voting.

In a democracy, one of the most basic rights a citizen has is their vote. A vote means they have a say in how things are run and who is in charge. The right to vote is valued. This may in part be a result of the history of voting in the United States. In the beginning, only free white males who owned land could vote. This was a small percentage of the population. Over time, others have fought for the right to vote. Today, the right belongs to most adult citizens.

Even so, concerns remain about keeping the right and access to voting open for all. In U.S. history, there are many examples of voter interference. Groups, including African Americans and women, have been kept from voting in various ways, big and small. Keeping voting open and fair for all is essential in a working democracy.

Amending the Constitution

A change to the U.S. Constitution is called an amendment. Through the years, there have been three key amendments to the Constitution that focus on voting rights. They are the 15th, 19th, and 26th amendments.

STEP 1 PRIMARIES AND CAUCUSES

People with similar ideas may belong to the same political party.

Candidates from each party campaign throughout the country to win the favor of their party members.

STEP 2 NATIONAL CONVENTIONS

In a caucus, party members select the best candidate through discussions and votes.

In a primary, party members vote for the best candidate to represent them.

Each party holds a national convention to select a nominee.

At each convention, the candidate chooses a running mate (vice president).

STEP 3 GENERAL ELECTION

The candidates campaign to win the support of the people.

People in every state vote for one president and vice president.

When people cast their votes, they are actually voting for a group of electors.

STEP 4 ELECTORAL COLLEGE

538 ELECTORAL VOTES

In the Electoral College system, each state gets a certain number of electors based on its representation in Congress.

Each elector casts one vote following the general election, and the candidate who gets more than half (270 votes) wins.

The newly elected president and vice president are inaugurated in January.

Voting Rights Act of 1965

One of the biggest battles in U.S. history was voting rights for African Americans. African Americans had the legal right to vote long before they actually could vote easily and safely. In 1870, the 15th Amendment changed their status. But in many places, they were kept from voting. States used **poll taxes** and **literacy tests** to keep African Americans away. Black citizens were threatened. They also knew voting could be dangerous for them.

A man registers to vote while others wait their turn.

Civil rights leaders Martin Luther King Jr. (center) and Coretta Scott King (right) cast their ballots.

The Voting Rights Act of 1965 opened the door for federal enforcement of the 15th Amendment. The federal government could make sure that states registered voters. They could enforce the right to vote at polls. Individual states could no longer place barriers on voters. The federal government could step in if the states did.

Language and Voting

The Voting Rights Act also calls for language assistance for many groups who are not able to speak or understand English well enough to vote.

Right or Responsibility?

Citizens have the opportunity and the right to be involved in government. Many would say they also have the responsibility. Democracies work best when people participate. In this way, the government can work for everyone.

The role of president is an important one. The president has a huge impact on the country and the world. If the people take part and vote, they can ensure that the impact is what they want and need.

American children today will vote for future presidents. Fortunately, they have tools to help them understand the candidates and how to vote. They can learn how elections work and the best ways to take part in them. They can get prepared. And then, they can cast their votes and make a difference.

There is one more big thing they can do. They can run for president, too!

Becoming President

What are the requirements to become president? A person must be a natural-born U.S. citizen, have lived in the United States for 14 years, and be at least 35 years old. The youngest person to assume the job of president was Theodore Roosevelt at age 42. He was vice president when President McKinley was killed. The youngest person to be elected was John F. Kennedy. He was 43 at his inauguration.

Young people demonstrate to support a cause.

COOL IT.

SYSTEM CHANGE

IF THE CLIMATE WAS a BANK, it WOULD already be $AVED

Think and Talk

In what ways can people in the United States make their voices heard?

Glossary

background check—research into a person's history

candidate—a person who is trying to be elected

inauguration—formal ceremony introducing someone, such as a president, into a job or a position

influenced—changed or had an impact

literacy tests—tests used to register people to vote by testing their reading ability, but often crafted in a way to ensure failure

platforms—official beliefs and goals of political parties or candidates

politicians—people who are active in government in official positions

polling—voting

polls—surveys in which a number of people are asked questions in order to assess what people think

poll taxes—fees charged to vote (no longer legal)

register—to add one's name and personal information to an official list

term—fixed amount of time

Index

Civics in Action

The president of the United States has an important and big job. American citizens get the chance to participate in hiring the right person for this job. But they usually only have a few candidates from which to choose. What if you had the power to attract the perfect candidate for president?

1. Consider what the must-have qualities are for the job.

2. Create an ad explaining your requirements.

3. Research and compare the current president to your perfect president.

4. Share your work!